ROURKE
SCIENCE
PROJECTS

SCIENCE IN FOOD

Authors: George and Shirley Coulter

Rourke Publications, Inc.
Vero Beach, Florida 32964

A book by Market Square Communications Incorporated
Pamela J.P. Schroeder, Editor

LIBRARY OF CONGRESS CATALOGING-IN-PUBLICATION DATA

Coulter, George, 1934-
    Science in food / by George and Shirley Coulter.
        p. cm. — (Rourke science projects)
    Includes index.
    ISBN 0-86625-518-4
    1. Food—Juvenile literature. 2. Science—Experiments—Juvenile literature.
[1. Science projects. 2. Science—Experiments. 3. Experiments. 4. Food.]
I. Coulter, Shirley, 1936-   . II. Title. III. Series.
TX355.C717 1995
540'.78—dc20
                                         94-49348
                                             CIP
                                             AC

Printed in the USA

TABLE OF CONTENTS

GET A TASTE OF BEING A SCIENTIST

Do you like to ask questions? Then you already have the makings of a real scientist!

Scientists ask questions about why things are the way they are, and then they search and test for the answers. Inside this book, you'll find questions about SCIENCE IN FOOD. Choose one—or more—that you want to investigate.

Even something as familiar as an after-school snack can be the source of scientific questions. Get yourself an apple, and take a bite out of science!

After scientists choose a question, they sometimes try to guess the answer, based on their experience. That guess is called a **hypothesis** (hii POTH uh siss). Then they experiment to find out if their hypothesis is right.

Once you choose your question, you'll start to experiment, using the steps written out for you. You'll be acting like a professional scientist, making careful **observations** (ahb zer VAY shunz), and writing down all your results in a **science log** (SII ens LAWG). Your notes are very important. You'll need to use them to make a display to share what you've learned with other people.

Please be careful while you're experimenting. Professional scientists are always aware of safety.

At the end of your experiment, you'll find—answers! Other people will believe your answers because you have scientific proof. However, you don't have to stop there. Your answer might lead to another question. Or you might want to find out about something else. Don't wait. Get a taste of being a scientist!

SCIENCE IN FOOD

Science is all around us. It's not just a separate subject you learn about in school. It's everywhere—in the air you breathe, the pictures you paint and the food you eat.

When you walk into a kitchen, you are really entering a **chemistry** (KEM iss tree) laboratory. You see stove-top burners and pans instead of Bunsen burners and bubbling test tubes, but the **chemical reactions** (KEM ik uhl ree AK shunz) that take place are the same.

Switch on the oven light or peer inside a pan. During cooking or baking, **liquids** (LI kwidz) change into **solids** (SAH lidz). You might also observe changes in color, texture, smell—and taste! These transformations might seem magical, but they really follow **physical laws** (FIZ i kul LAWZ) of science.

Everything about food involves science. The planting, growing and harvesting of food, the transportation and packaging of food, and the marketing and preparation of food all depend on the ideas and materials of science.

Eating and digesting food also involves science—**biology** (bii AHL uh jee). Food is necessary for you to fuel all the **biological processes** (bii ah LAH ji kuhl PRAH sess iz) you need to keep on living. So the next time you sit down to a meal or catch a quick snack, remember—science is a part of you and all you do.

HOW CAN YOU TEST FOODS FOR VITAMIN C?

Did you ever drink orange juice to try to keep from getting a cold? Many people believe that the **vitamin C** (VII teh min SEE) in orange juice can prevent or cure colds.

Vitamin C is necessary to keep healthy. You can get vitamin C if you eat the right fruits and vegetables. Some people even take vitamin C tablets. Where are you getting your vitamin C?

What To Do

Be very careful with the iodine **solution** (suh LOO shun). Do not do taste tests during this experiment. Iodine is poisonous and can stain your clothes.

Step 1 First you'll make a liquid vitamin C **indicator** (IN deh kay tuhr). Add 1/4 teaspoon (1 ml) of liquid laundry **starch** (STARCH) to 2 cups (480 ml) of tap water. Carefully pour this **mixture** (MIKS chur) into your 20-ounce (600-ml) plastic bottle. (Using a funnel may help prevent spilling.) Put on the cap and shake the bottle.

Then, use the medicine dropper to add 10 drops of iodine solution. (Wash out your medicine dropper after every use by removing the bulb and washing it and the glass tube under warm, running water.) Close the bottle and shake again.

What You Need

✓ 500-mg or 250-mg vitamin C tablets (available in drug stores)
✓ medicine dropper (available in drug stores)
✓ liquid laundry starch
✓ iodine solution—tincture of iodine (available in drug stores)
✓ 20-ounce (600-ml) plastic bottle (soda pop bottle)
✓ tap water
✓ several small, disposable plastic or paper cups
✓ plastic measuring spoons

Add the substance you are testing to the vitamin C indicator one drop at a time. Record the number of drops it takes to turn the indicator clear.

Your vitamin C indicator will only be good for a few days. Make sure to shake your bottle each time before using the indicator. Also, be sure to use this indicator only to test foods. Other substances may change color, but that will not necessarily prove they contain vitamin C.

Step 2 Now, make a vitamin C solution. **Dissolve** (diz AWLV) a 500-mg vitamin C tablet in 8 ounces (240 ml) of water—or a 250-mg tablet in 4 ounces (120 ml) of water—and set it aside.

Step 3 Measure 1 tablespoon (15 ml) of your vitamin C indicator into a disposable cup. Then carefully add five drops of your vitamin C solution to the indicator in the cup. Notice any changes and record your **observations** in your **science log.** The next time you see this reaction, you'll know you've found vitamin C.

Step 4 Measure 1 tablespoon (15 ml) of vitamin C indicator into another disposable cup. Fill your medicine dropper with orange juice and add it to your indicator one drop at a time, until you see a change. How many drops did it take? Write your observations in your log.

Step 5 Repeat Step 4 using other juices. (Remember to clean your medicine dropper after each use.) You can test solid foods by blending them with water to make a solution before adding them to the indicator. Label each cup with the juice or food you tested.

If you do not see your indicator change after adding 50 drops, the solution you are testing probably has no vitamin C.

Make a chart or **bar graph** (BAR GRAF) of all the foods you tested and how many drops it took to change the indicator.

Is This What Happened?

Step 1: When you added the liquid starch to the water it turned slightly cloudy. Adding the iodine solution turned the mixture purple, or blue-black.

Step 3: Your indicator should have turned colorless.

Step 4: Your indicator should have turned colorless, but it may have taken more than five drops of orange juice.

Step 5: Most juices you tested probably caused your vitamin C indicator to lose its color.

Your vitamin C indicator will only work for a few days. Make sure to shake the bottle each time before using it. Remember to be careful—the iodine solution in your indicator is poisonous.

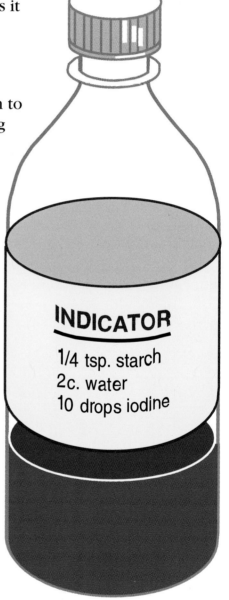

INDICATOR
1/4 tsp. starch
2c. water
10 drops iodine

Why?

By itself, iodine solution is a brownish color. When you mix it with starch, a **chemical reaction** takes place to form a new blue-black liquid—your vitamin C indicator.

Mixing vitamin C—also known as **ascorbic acid** (uh SKOR bik A sid)—with your indicator causes another chemical reaction. You are actually creating two new substances—hydroascorbic (hii droh uh SKOR bik) acid and hydroiodic (hii droh ii AH dik) acid. Both of these acids are colorless, so your indicator loses its color. Adding foods that contain more vitamin C helps the reaction happen faster. The less drops you need, the more vitamin C is present.

The next time you feel sick, if you're tired of orange juice, what will you reach for?

Vitamin C is an important part of our everyday diets. How much vitamin C is in the foods you eat?

WHAT IS THE CHEMISTRY OF HARD CANDY?

Have you ever said "no" to a piece of hard candy? After a while, it melts in your mouth, but how does it stick together in the first place?

Thanks to the science of **solutions,** we can tickle our taste buds with all kinds of sweet flavors.

What To Do

Step 1 In a drinking glass, mix together 1 teaspoon of sugar, two drops of food coloring and a drop of flavoring. Stir well and taste. Write down your **observations** in your **science log.**

Step 2 Spray the inside of your pie tin or cake pan with a non-stick vegetable spray and set it aside.

Measure the following ingredients into your cooking pot: 1 3/4 cups (420 ml) of sugar, 1/2 cup (120 ml) of corn syrup and 1/2 cup (120 ml) of water.

Step 3 Ask an adult to help you through the next steps. The stove, pan, thermometer and candy **mixture** will be extremely hot. Place the cooking pot on a stove burner set to "high." Stir the mixture until it boils. Then stop stirring and let the mixture heat to 300°F (150°C), according to your candy thermometer.

What You Need

- ✓ sugar
- ✓ corn syrup
- ✓ water
- ✓ liquid food coloring
- ✓ liquid flavoring of your choice (like vanilla, almond, peppermint, etc.)
- ✓ measuring cup
- ✓ teaspoon
- ✓ drinking glass
- ✓ cooking pan—1 quart or larger
- ✓ non-stick vegetable spray
- ✓ 9-inch (23-cm) aluminum pie pan or 8-inch (20-cm) square cake pan
- ✓ stove
- ✓ candy thermometer
- ✓ adult to help

After your candy stops boiling, stir in 1/2 teaspoon of food coloring and 1/2 teaspoon of flavoring. Then carefully pour it into the pie tin or cake pan you prepared in Step 2.

Step 4 Remove the pot from the burner and let it cool. When the mixture stops boiling, add 1/2 teaspoon (2.5 ml) or less of food coloring and 1/2 teaspoon (2.5 ml) or more of flavoring. Use a spoon with a long handle to stir until the mixture is the same color all the way through. Then pour the mixture into the pie tin or cake pan you prepared in Step 2.

Step 5 When the mixture has cooled completely, break the candy into pieces. Cover the pan with a clean towel and gently bang the pan on a table top, or hit it with a hammer.

Describe your candy in your science log. How does it taste? How does it compare to the solution you made in Step 1? Save some of your candy for your final display.

Hard candy is colorful, sweet, transparent and tasty—a perfect solution for a sweet tooth.

Is This What Happened?

Step 1: The mixture in the glass was the color of the food coloring, but still clear enough to see through, like water. It tasted sweet, like sugar, but with the slight flavor of the flavoring you added.

Step 5: Just like the solution in Step 1, your hard candy was the color of the food coloring, but still clear enough to see through. It should taste sweet, but with the flavor of the flavoring you added. The only difference is that this mixture is a **solid.**

Why?

Both the colored, sweet **liquid** in the glass and the solid candy are solutions. Each part—each ingredient—of a solution is mixed evenly throughout the whole solution. A piece of candy from one part of your pan will look, taste, smell and feel like a piece from any other part of the pan.

Solutions are great examples of cooperation. A solution has the **properties** (PRAHP er teez) of all of its parts. Both solutions contain food coloring, water, sugar and flavoring. So, both solutions are colorful, clear, sweet and tasty.

The hard candy turned hard because it is mostly made up of solid sugar. A lot of the water you added evaporated, or turned into steam, as the candy boiled. Since there is more solid than liquid in this solution, it acts more like a solid.

Now if you ever have a lack of candy, you've got the perfect solution!

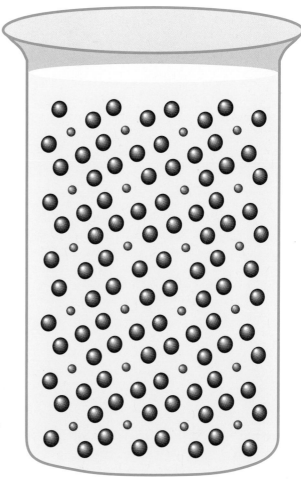

All the parts of a solution are spread evenly throughout the solution. So, a solution has the properties of all of its parts.

WHY IS BAKING POWDER USED IN BAKING?

At your house, do you make pancakes and waffles from scratch, or do you use a mix? What about cakes and cookies? Either way, somewhere in your recipe, you need to have **baking powder** (BAY king POW duhr).

In this experiment, you'll get a rise out of the **chemistry** of baking powder.

What You Need

✓ baking powder
✓ sifted all-purpose flour
✓ salt
✓ shortening
✓ milk
✓ measuring cup
✓ 2 mixing bowls
✓ baking sheet or cookie sheet
✓ cookie cutter or drinking glass
✓ rolling pin

What To Do

Step 1 Preheat your oven to 450°F (232°C). Lightly grease a baking sheet and set it aside until you are ready to bake.

Step 2 In a mixing bowl, mix together 1 cup (240 ml) of all-purpose flour, 1 1/2 teaspoons (8 ml) of baking powder, 1/4 teaspoon (1 ml) of salt, and 2 tablespoons (30 ml) of shortening. When this is well mixed, add 1/3 cup (80 ml) of whole milk and stir into a soft dough.

Step 3 Place your dough on a floured board or counter, and knead it for about 1/2 minute. Then use a rolling pin to roll the dough until it is about 1/2 to 3/4 inch (1.5 to 3 cm) thick. Cut circles with a cookie cutter or drinking glass.

Step 4 Put your dough circles on the baking sheet you prepared in Step 1. Bake at 450°F (232°C) for about 12 minutes. Then, wearing an oven mitt, remove them from the oven and allow them to cool a few minutes. Write all of your **observations** down in your **science log.** How do the biscuits look, smell, taste and feel? What happens if you add strawberry jam? You may want to save a sample for your final display.

Step 5 Repeat Step 1 through Step 4 *except* don't add any baking powder. What differences do you notice? Write everything in your science log.

Knead the dough for about 1/2 minute. Kneading will help you shape the dough into a ball that you can roll.

Is This What Happened?

Step 4: The biscuits should have raised up and been fluffy. The texture and taste should be just as you'd expect, even better with jam.

Step 5: These so-called biscuits should have been flat. The insides may not have been cooked all the way through. If you dropped one, or tasted one, it probably reminded you more of a hockey puck than a biscuit.

Sticky gluten traps carbon dioxide gas in the biscuit as it's baking. Carbon dioxide bubbles give soda pop its fizz, and biscuits their fluff!

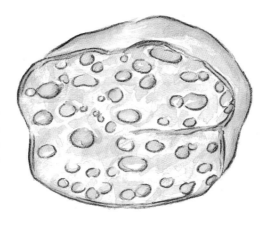

Baking powder makes biscuits rise to the occasion.

Why?

Baking powder is a mixture of sodium bicarbonate (SOH dee um bii KAR buh nuht), tartaric acid (tar TAR ik A sid) and cornstarch. It is the **chemical reaction** between the sodium bicarbonate and tartaric acid that we want to pay attention to.

With the heat of the oven and the moisture from the milk, the sodium bicarbonate and the tartaric acid react to form **carbon dioxide** (KAR bun dii OKS iid) gas—the same carbon dioxide your body makes when you exhale, or breathe out. The carbon dioxide forms gas bubbles that rise within the dough, just like the bubbles you see rising in a glass of soda pop.

The flour contains **gluten** (GLOO tehn), a sticky substance **elastic** (ee LASS tik) enough to expand and trap the gas bubbles in the dough. As the dough bakes, it hardens around the gas bubbles to form a **solid foam** (FOHM)—a fluffy biscuit. Since there was no baking powder in your second set of biscuits, carbon dioxide couldn't form, and your experiment fell flat!

HOW CAN YOU USE MILK TO MAKE GLUE?

In your lifetime you have probably already used a least a gallon of white glue. In school, at home, in crafts classes, at summer camp—those white bottles are pretty familiar.

However, did you know that you could make all the glue you could ever need right at home in your own kitchen?

What To Do

Step 1 Measure out 6 ounces (180 ml) skim milk into a measuring cup. Add 2 ounces (60 ml) of white vinegar.

Ask an adult to help you pour this **mixture** into a sauce pan and heat it on a stove. Be careful not to boil it. Wait until you see clumps of white **solid** appear. Then remove the pan from the stove.

Step 2 Make a filter using a double layer of paper towels. Use the diagram on page 19 to show you how. Or, if you're using cheesecloth, drape the cheesecloth over the rim of the funnel and push it in. Make sure some of the cloth remains outside the cup so you can hold it in place. (You may want to place a funnel underneath your filter to keep it from slipping.)

Step 3 Slowly, pour the mixture from the pan into the filter. Make sure all of the solid gets into the filter. Let the mixture run through the filter until all the **liquid** is in your glass.

Rinse the solid that is left with water, and filter again. Squeeze any liquid left in the filter out. What is the solid like? Rub some between your thumb and finger. Record all of your **observations** in your **science log.**

What You Need

✓ skim milk
✓ white vinegar
✓ baking soda
✓ measuring cup
✓ measuring spoons
✓ sauce pan
✓ stove
✓ cheesecloth or heavy-duty paper towels
✓ large, plastic drinking glass
✓ spoon or knife for stirring

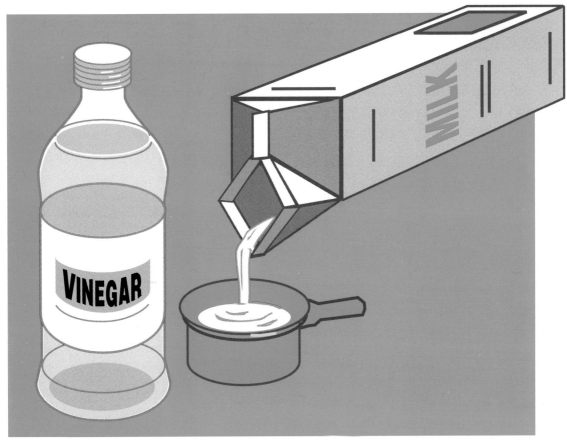

Measure 6 ounces (180 ml) of skim milk and 2 ounces (60 ml) of white vinegar, and mix them together.

Step 4 Measure 3 tablespoons (45 ml) of hot water into a measuring cup and add 1 1/2 teaspoons (8 ml) of baking soda to the water. As you stir this mixture, add the white solid. Keep stirring until all the lumps have disappeared. What is happening in the cup? Write down what you see.

Step 5 Smear this new mixture on a piece of paper. Smooth another piece of paper over the top and press it down. Set it aside for at least an hour. Then try to pull the pieces of paper apart. What happens? Record all of your observations. Save your glue for your final display in a container that has a top, or that can be covered with plastic wrap so it doesn't dry up.

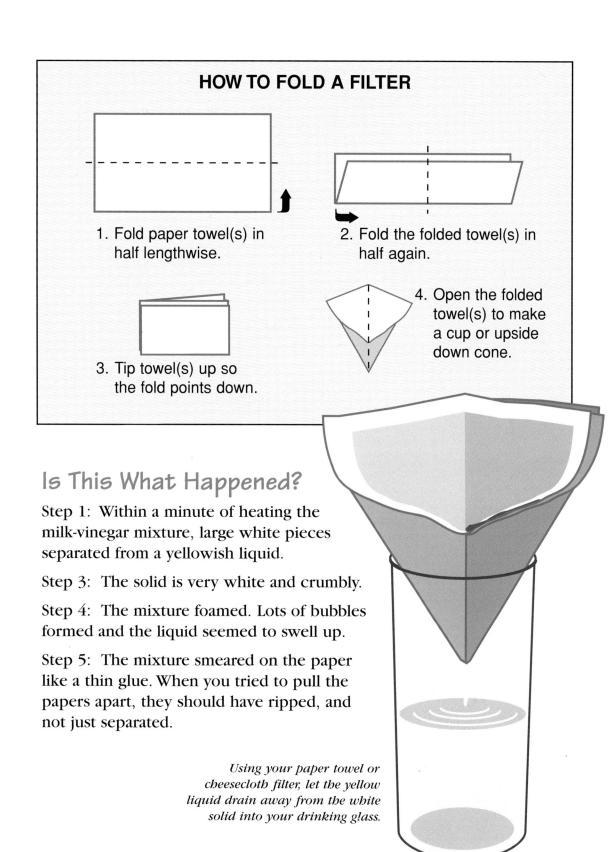

HOW TO FOLD A FILTER

1. Fold paper towel(s) in half lengthwise.

2. Fold the folded towel(s) in half again.

3. Tip towel(s) up so the fold points down.

4. Open the folded towel(s) to make a cup or upside down cone.

Is This What Happened?

Step 1: Within a minute of heating the milk-vinegar mixture, large white pieces separated from a yellowish liquid.

Step 3: The solid is very white and crumbly.

Step 4: The mixture foamed. Lots of bubbles formed and the liquid seemed to swell up.

Step 5: The mixture smeared on the paper like a thin glue. When you tried to pull the papers apart, they should have ripped, and not just separated.

Using your paper towel or cheesecloth filter, let the yellow liquid drain away from the white solid into your drinking glass.

Why?

When you added the vinegar to the milk and heated it in Step 1, a **chemical reaction** took place. The milk soured and separated into a white solid—the curds, and the liquid part—the whey. Remember Little Miss Muppet?

In Step 4, you created another chemical reaction. The baking soda reacted with any vinegar still left on the curds to form **carbon dioxide** gas. That was the bubbles you observed.

Chemists call the white curds you used **casein** (kay SEEN). Casein is a **protein** (PRO teen) found in milk. Casein glue works because the **molecules** (MAHL i kyoolz) in the glue are strongly attracted to the molecules in the objects the glue is holding together. The white glue you buy off the shelf is a refined form of the casein glue you just made. With a little scientific know-how, you can turn your kitchen into a glue factory!

The casein glue you made is very close to the glue you can buy off the shelf. Glue works because the molecules in the glue are strongly attracted to the molecules in the objects the glue is holding together.

HOW CAN YOU MAKE ICE CREAM WITHOUT A FREEZER?

"I scream, you scream, we all scream for ice cream!" Ice cream is a cool, creamy treat—and hard to pass up.

Thanks to a process called **freezing point depression** (FREEZ ing POYNT dee PREH shun), you can make ice cream any time you have a taste for it—even on a hot summer afternoon.

What To Do

Step 1 In a mixing bowl, mix together 1/2 cup (120 ml) whipping cream, 4 tablespoons sugar and 1/4 teaspoon of vanilla extract. Stir until all of the sugar is **dissolved.**

Pour this **mixture** into a clean baby food jar. Leave about 1 inch (2.5 cm) empty at the top of the jar. Then cap it tightly.

Step 2 Cover the bottom of a large coffee can or large plastic container with ice. Pour a layer of rock salt over the ice. Place the baby food jar in the center of the container. Then, layer ice and salt until the container is completely full. Fit the lid on the container tightly.

Step 3 Roll the container back and forth for four minutes. Then rest for one minute, and roll again for four minutes. Keep repeating this until you reach 20 minutes. You may want to wear gloves. The container will get very cold. What happens to the outside of the container? Write your **observations** in your **science log.**

Step 4 Remove the baby food jar from the container and wipe it dry with paper towels. Open the jar and use a knife to scrape the inside of the jar, mixing any **solid** and the **liquid** together.

What You Need

- ✓ large coffee can with a lid or large plastic container with lid
- ✓ 6-ounce (180-ml) baby food jar with lid
- ✓ whipping cream
- ✓ sugar
- ✓ vanilla extract
- ✓ ice cubes
- ✓ water softener salt or rock salt (not pellets)
- ✓ paper towels
- ✓ knife
- ✓ small mixing bowl

Step 5 Recap the jar, put it back in its place in the container, and roll it around for another 20 minutes. Then remove the baby food jar, open it and observe what's inside. What does it look, smell, feel and taste like? Record your observations. You may want to store some of your ice cream in a freezer or refrigerator so people can sample your work as you display your final project.

Seal the mixture you made in Step 1 in a clean baby food jar, and place the jar in the center of a large container. Layer ice and salt around the jar until your container is full.

You might want to wear gloves when rolling your container. You don't want to get frostbite!

Is This What Happened?

Step 3: Frost formed on the outside of the container.

Step 5: The contents of the jar should have blended into a solid, and tasted just like ice cream!

Ice cream is so cool, you can make it without a refrigerator!

Why?

At 32°F (0°C), two things happen—water freezes and ice melts. Ice cream will not form unless the temperature is several degrees below 32°F (0°C). So how can you create freezing temperatures on a hot summer day?

First, you need ice. But even ice melts on a hot day. By adding salt to your ice, you actually lowered the temperature of the ice-water mixture (and water's freezing temperature). Your ice-salt mixture may have gotten as cold as 5°F—that's ⁻15°C! The process of adding salt (or any substance) to water (or any liquid) to lower the freezing temperature is called *freezing point depression.*

The baby food jar and the mixture inside lost heat to the ice-salt mixture, until they were both the same temperature, and the mixture froze. With freezing point depression, you can beat the heat and make a cool treat!

HOW IS A BOTTLE OF SODA POP LIKE YOUR STOMACH?

What happens to food after you eat it? Our bodies can't use food the way it is. We have to break it down so it can move through the bloodstream to get to every hungry **cell** (SELL). This process is called **digestion** (dii JES chun).

What To Do

Step 1 Chew a soda cracker for two full minutes. (This might be harder than you think.) Try not to swallow any, or spit any out. How did the cracker taste when you first started chewing? How did it taste after two minutes? What was the texture? Write all your **observations** in your **science log.**

Step 2 Pour 1/2 cup (120 ml) of water into a wide-mouth bottle. Roll a piece of hamburger into a ball about 1/2 inch (1.3 cm) in diameter, and put it in the bottle. Then cap and label it. Be sure to wash your hands after handling the raw hamburger.

This jar filled with water is your *control.* Scientists use the control to compare the results during their experiments.

What You Need

✓ unsalted, unsweetened soda crackers
✓ fresh hamburger
✓ meat tenderizer that contains papain
✓ 3 small, wide-mouth bottles with caps
✓ cola
✓ water

Step 3 Pour 1/2 cup (120 ml) of water into another wide-mouth bottle. Add 2 tablespoons of meat tenderizer, cap the bottle and shake it until the tenderizer is **dissolved.** Then put in a hamburger ball as in Step 2, and recap and label the bottle.

Step 4 Pour 1/2 cup (120 ml) cup of cola into a wide-mouth bottle. Put in a hamburger ball as in Step 2, and cap and label the bottle.

Step 5 Set the bottles where they will not be disturbed. Check them after a few hours and write all your observations in your science log. Check them again after 24 hours (1 day), and again after 48 hours (2 days).

Is This What Happened?

Step 1: When you started chewing, the cracker should have tasted bland and had a rough, dry texture. After two minutes, the cracker should have changed completely—into mush. The liquid in your mouth should have tasted sweet.

Step 5: The meat in the water may have changed color a little.

However, the meat in the tenderizer solution definitely changed color, and it should have looked ragged. Fibers of white material may have been hanging from the meat. Also, your hamburger ball may have come apart.

You may have noticed fizzing when the meat was dropped into the cola, and it may still have been fizzing when you checked back a few hours later. After 24 hours, the meat should have been in pieces, and the cola might be a slightly different color. (This change in color does not have to do with digestion. It's another **chemical reaction** happening in the bottle at the same time.) After 48 hours a good word to describe your hamburger ball is *disintegrated!*

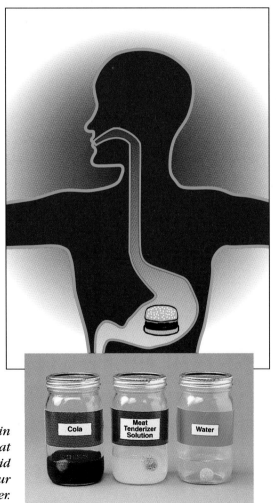

After Step 4, you'll have a hamburger ball in three different liquids—water, meat tenderizer dissolved in water, and cola. Acid in the cola works like the acid in your stomach on the hamburger.

26

ENZYME BREAKING DOWN PROTEIN CHAIN

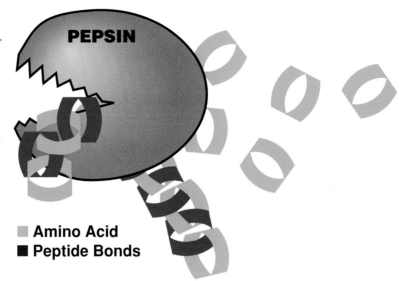

Protein molecules are really long chains of amino acids linked by peptide bonds. An enzyme called pepsin works in our stomachs to break down protein into smaller, simpler amino acids.

■ **Amino Acid**
■ **Peptide Bonds**

Why?

When you put the cracker in your mouth in Step 1, you started digesting it right away! Your teeth broke the cracker into small bits, and an **enzyme** (EN ziim) in your saliva, called ptyalin, started its work. Ptyalin changes large **starch molecules** into smaller and simpler sugar molecules. That's why the cracker started to taste sweet instead of salty.

After you swallow a cracker, or any other food, it slides into your stomach where more enzymes go to work. The meat tenderizer contained an enzyme very much like pepsin—which we have in our stomachs. Pepsin breaks down **protein,** so your hamburger balls didn't stand a chance. The white fibers you saw were fat. Pepsin only works on protein, so the fat was left behind.

The plastic bottle, meat and cola work like a model of digestion. Looking through a bottle of cola is like looking through the wall of your stomach. Why? All carbonated sodas—including cola—contain **carbonic acid** (kar BON ik A sid), and some contain citric acid. Your stomach contains hydrochloric acid (hii droh KLOR ik A sid). When you plop a hamburger ball into your cola bottle, or into your stomach, the acids start to break down the meat fibers, and the meat becomes tender. The cola in your experiment actually started to digest the meat!

HOW TO DISPLAY YOUR PROJECT

When you finish your project, your teacher may ask you to share it with your class or show it at a science fair. Professional scientists often show their work to other people. Here are some tips on how to display your project.

Many students show their projects with a three-board, free-standing display. Before you start putting everything together, make a sketch of how you would like your display to look. This is the best time to make changes.

Tip #1

Make your headline stand out with a catchy phrase, a sentence or even a question

The title of your project should attract people's attention. It could be one or two words—a catchy phrase, a sentence or even a question. Use the largest lettering for your title. In your display, you should also state the scientific problem you were trying to solve. Use a question, like the chapter titles in this book, or state your problem in the form of a **hypothesis.**

If you have a computer of your own, or can use one at school, they work great for lettering. Or, you can neatly print on a white sheet of paper, and border your lettering with colored construction paper to make it stand out.

You'll also need to leave room to display the most important part of your project—your results. Show any photographs, drawings, charts, graphs or tables—anything that will help to explain what you've learned. You can use

Tip #2

Use color on graphs and charts

black marker to make tables and charts, and colored marker for graphs. If you're handy with a computer, you might try to make your graphs and charts with a computer program!

Once you have all the pieces, tape everything into place. Follow the sketch you drew. Using tape will let you rearrange things until your display looks exactly how you want it. Then glue the pieces permanently.

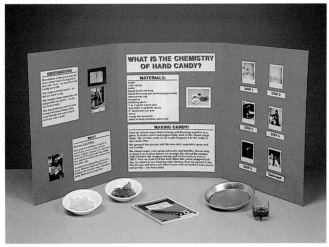

Tip #3
Label everything clearly

As part of your exhibit, you'll want to include your **science log** and final report, along with any equipment you used, or models you made. Make sure your report is easy to read—neatly printed or typed. Be sure to label everything clearly.

Finally, you'll want to be able to tell people about your project. Practice what you want to say beforehand as many times as you can. Tell your parents, a friend, or even your dog about it. Then when a teacher or judge asks you about your project, you'll know what to say. You can share what you've discovered, and show that science really is part of everyone's life. After all, you've just become a real scientist!

Sharing your results is an important part of being a scientist. A well-organized display will make explaining what you've learned easier.

GLOSSARY

ascorbic acid (uh SKOR bik A sid) – the chemical name for vitamin C

biological processes (bii ah LAH ji kuhl PRAH sess iz) – activities carried out by living things such as getting and using energy, growing, reacting and reproducing

biology (bii AHL uh jee) – the study of living things

carbon dioxide (KAR buhn dii OKS iid) – a non-poisonous gas made up of carbon and oxygen

carbonic acid (kar BON ik A sid) – a weak acid formed when carbon dioxide gas dissolves in water; found in soda pop

casein (kay SEEN) – a mixture of proteins found in the curds of milk; used to make glues, plastics, paints and cheese

cell (SELL) – the smallest living part of any living thing

chemical reaction (KEM ik uhl ree AK shun) – changes in matter; how substances turn into other substances

chemistry (KEM iss tree) – the study of matter—what things are made of; how it's classified, how it's put together and the changes it goes through

digestion (dii JES chun) – how living things break down food into simple substances that their cells can use to create energy

dissolve (diz AWLV) – to break down one substance in another substance so that all parts are equal throughout; to go into solution

elastic (ee LASS tik) – able to be stretched, and then returned to the original shape

enzymes (EN ziimz) – chemicals in living things that help bring about chemical reactions; some enzymes help digest food by breaking it down into simpler substances

foam (FOHM) – a mixture of a gas in a liquid or solid; bubbles trapped in a substance

freezing point depression (FREEZ ing POYNT dee PREH shun) – lowering the freezing temperature of a substance; dissolving something in water to lower its freezing temperature

gluten (GLOO tehn) – a mixture of proteins found in wheat flour; a sticky elastic material that can trap gas

hypothesis (hii POTH uh siss) - a possible answer to a scientific question; sometimes called an educated guess because scientists use what they *already* know to guess how the experiment will turn out

indicator (IN deh kay tuhr) - a substance that changes color in the presence of other specific substances

liquid (LI kwid) - a state of matter—what things are made of—that takes up a definite amount of space, but does not have definite shape; liquids take on the shape of their containers

mixture (MIKS chur) - two or more substances that are not chemically combined; a mixture has the properties of all of its parts

molecule (MAHL i kyool) - the smallest part of a substance (element or compound) that has the properties of that substance; H_2 represents a molecule of hydrogen (an element), H_2O represents a molecule of water (a compound)

observation (ahb zer VAY shun) - information gathered by carefully using your senses; seeing, hearing, touching, smelling and tasting

physical laws (FIZ i kul LAWZ) - rules that scientists have found that describe how nonliving things work

properties (PROP er teez) - how a substance looks, tastes, smells, sounds, feels and reacts to other things; how we identify a substance

protein (PRO teen) - a substance containing nitrogen that is found in all living things; an important part of the foods we eat

science log (SII ens LAWG) - a notebook that includes the title of your project, the date you started, your list of materials, procedures you followed with dates and times, your observations and results

solid (SAH lid) - a state of matter—what things are made of—that takes up space and has a definite shape, or fixed form

solution (suh LOO shun) - a mixture in which all parts are mixed evenly throughout; a solution will not settle out and cannot be separated by filtering

starch (STARCH) - one of a group of carbohydrate foods; found in breads, crackers, cookies and cakes

vitamin C (VII teh min SEE) - ascorbic acid, a substance our bodies need to function properly